Jig and Jog

C000184950

Written by Teresa Heapy

Collins

We jig and jog on the mats.

3

I can toss this rod.

pink

I run. I am quick!

I hang on top.

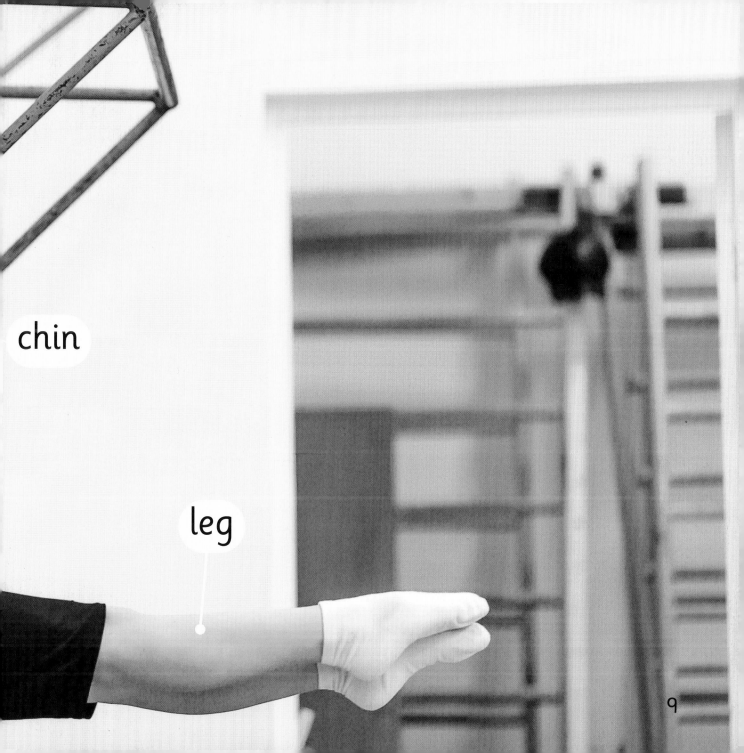

chin

leg

9

I sink and kick.

I push off. Thud!

We jog.

We will get fit.

/qu/

14

15

 Review: After reading

Use your assessment from hearing the children read to choose any GPCs, words or tricky words that need additional practice.

Read 1: Decoding

- Practise reading words that contain new phonemes (letter sounds).
- Say the sounds in the words below.

  th/u/d   s/i/nk   h/a/ng

- Ask the children to repeat the sounds and then say the word.
- Look at the "I spy sounds" pages (14–15) together. How many words can the children point out from the picture that contain the /qu/ sound (e.g. *quench, quick, queen, quiet*) or the /nk/ sound? (e.g. *drink, think, pink*)

Read 2: Prosody

- Model reading each page with expression to the children. After you have read each page, ask the children to have a go at reading with expression.

Read 3: Comprehension

- For every question ask the children how they know the answer. Ask:
  o What are some of the things the children are doing? (e.g. *aerobics, gymnastics, dancing*)
  o What was the dancer holding up? (*a rod with a ribbon*)
  o Can you think of any other ways to keep fit? (e.g. *running, swimming*)
  o If you were writing a book about keeping fit, what would be in it?